# THIS RECIPE NOTEBOOK BELONGS TO

_____

**OrangeBlueberry**

All rights reserved.

No portion of this book may be reproduced in any form without permission from the publisher, except as permitted by U.S. copyright law.

# TABLE OF CONTENTS

RECIPE　　　　　　　　　　　　　　　　　　　　　　　PAGE

# TABLE OF CONTENTS

RECIPE

PAGE

# TABLE OF CONTENTS

**RECIPE**                                                  **PAGE**

# TABLE OF CONTENTS

RECIPE                                                                                      PAGE

# TABLE OF CONTENTS

RECIPE  PAGE

Bon appétit!

# Recipe:

**PREP TIME**

**COOKING TIME**

## INGREDIENTS

## DIRECTIONS

**NOTES**

# Recipe: _____

**PREP TIME** .................... **COOKING TIME** ....................

## INGREDIENTS

## DIRECTIONS

## NOTES

# Recipe: _____

PREP TIME ......................... COOKING TIME .........................

## INGREDIENTS

## DIRECTIONS

## NOTES

# Recipe:

**PREP TIME**

**COOKING TIME**

## INGREDIENTS

## DIRECTIONS

## NOTES

# Recipe: _____

**PREP TIME** ............................................  **COOKING TIME** ............................................

## INGREDIENTS

## DIRECTIONS

## NOTES

# Recipe: _____

**PREP TIME** .................... **COOKING TIME** ....................

## INGREDIENTS

## DIRECTIONS

## NOTES

# Recipe:

PREP TIME

COOKING TIME

## INGREDIENTS

## DIRECTIONS

## NOTES

# Recipe: _____

PREP TIME .................... COOKING TIME ....................

## INGREDIENTS

## DIRECTIONS

## NOTES

# Recipe: _____

**PREP TIME** .......................................... **COOKING TIME** ..........................................

## INGREDIENTS

## DIRECTIONS

## NOTES

# Recipe: _____

PREP TIME .................... COOKING TIME ....................

## INGREDIENTS

## DIRECTIONS

## NOTES

Recipe: _____

PREP TIME ............................ COOKING TIME ............................

INGREDIENTS

DIRECTIONS

NOTES

# Recipe: _____

PREP TIME ............................................. COOKING TIME .............................................

## INGREDIENTS

## DIRECTIONS

## NOTES

# Recipe: _____

**PREP TIME** ................................  **COOKING TIME** ................................

## INGREDIENTS

## DIRECTIONS

## NOTES

# Recipe: _____

PREP TIME ..................... COOKING TIME .....................

## INGREDIENTS

## DIRECTIONS

## NOTES

# Recipe:

**PREP TIME**

**COOKING TIME**

## INGREDIENTS

## DIRECTIONS

## NOTES

# Recipe: _____

PREP TIME .................... COOKING TIME ....................

## INGREDIENTS

## DIRECTIONS

## NOTES

# Recipe:

**PREP TIME**

**COOKING TIME**

## INGREDIENTS

## DIRECTIONS

## NOTES

# Recipe:

**PREP TIME** .................... **COOKING TIME** ....................

## INGREDIENTS

## DIRECTIONS

## NOTES

# Recipe:

**PREP TIME**

**COOKING TIME**

## INGREDIENTS

## DIRECTIONS

## NOTES

# Recipe: _____

PREP TIME ..................................  COOKING TIME ..................................

## INGREDIENTS

## DIRECTIONS

## NOTES

# Recipe: _____

PREP TIME .................... COOKING TIME ....................

## INGREDIENTS

## DIRECTIONS

## NOTES

**Recipe:** _____

PREP TIME ............................................... COOKING TIME ...............................................

## INGREDIENTS

## DIRECTIONS

## NOTES

# Recipe: _____

**PREP TIME** ..........................    **COOKING TIME** ..........................

## INGREDIENTS

## DIRECTIONS

## NOTES

# Recipe: _____

PREP TIME ............................................

COOKING TIME ............................................

## INGREDIENTS

## DIRECTIONS

## NOTES

# Recipe:

**PREP TIME**

**COOKING TIME**

## INGREDIENTS

## DIRECTIONS

**NOTES**

# Recipe: _____

**PREP TIME** ........................  **COOKING TIME** ........................

## INGREDIENTS

## DIRECTIONS

## NOTES

# Recipe: _____

**PREP TIME** ......................................... **COOKING TIME** .........................................

## INGREDIENTS

## DIRECTIONS

## NOTES

# Recipe: _____

**PREP TIME** .................................... **COOKING TIME** ....................................

## INGREDIENTS

## DIRECTIONS

## NOTES

# Recipe: _____

**PREP TIME** ................................    **COOKING TIME** ................................

## INGREDIENTS

## DIRECTIONS

## NOTES

# Recipe: _____

PREP TIME .................... COOKING TIME ....................

## INGREDIENTS

## DIRECTIONS

## NOTES

# Recipe:

**PREP TIME**

**COOKING TIME**

## INGREDIENTS

## DIRECTIONS

**NOTES**

# Recipe: _____

PREP TIME .................... COOKING TIME ....................

## INGREDIENTS

## DIRECTIONS

## NOTES

# Recipe:

**PREP TIME**

**COOKING TIME**

## INGREDIENTS

## DIRECTIONS

## NOTES

# Recipe:

PREP TIME

COOKING TIME

## INGREDIENTS

## DIRECTIONS

## NOTES

# Recipe: _____

**PREP TIME** ..........................  **COOKING TIME** ..........................

## INGREDIENTS

## DIRECTIONS

## NOTES

# Recipe: _____

**PREP TIME** ..................................  **COOKING TIME** ..................................

## INGREDIENTS

## DIRECTIONS

## NOTES

Recipe: _____

PREP TIME .................... COOKING TIME ....................

INGREDIENTS

DIRECTIONS

NOTES

# Recipe: _____

**PREP TIME** .................................. **COOKING TIME** ..................................

## INGREDIENTS

## DIRECTIONS

## NOTES

# Recipe:

**PREP TIME**

**COOKING TIME**

## INGREDIENTS

## DIRECTIONS

## NOTES

# Recipe: _____

PREP TIME ................................

COOKING TIME ................................

## INGREDIENTS

## DIRECTIONS

## NOTES

# Recipe: _____

PREP TIME .................... COOKING TIME ....................

## INGREDIENTS

## DIRECTIONS

## NOTES

# Recipe: _____

**PREP TIME** ....................................

**COOKING TIME** ....................................

## INGREDIENTS

## DIRECTIONS

## NOTES

# Recipe:

**PREP TIME**

**COOKING TIME**

## INGREDIENTS

## DIRECTIONS

## NOTES

# Recipe: _____

**PREP TIME** .................... **COOKING TIME** ....................

## INGREDIENTS

## DIRECTIONS

## NOTES

**Recipe:** _____

PREP TIME ................

COOKING TIME ................

INGREDIENTS

DIRECTIONS

NOTES

# Recipe: _____

**PREP TIME** .................................................

**COOKING TIME** ...............................................

## INGREDIENTS

## DIRECTIONS

## NOTES

# Recipe:

**PREP TIME**

**COOKING TIME**

## INGREDIENTS

## DIRECTIONS

## NOTES

# Recipe:

**PREP TIME**

**COOKING TIME**

## INGREDIENTS

## DIRECTIONS

## NOTES

# Recipe:

**PREP TIME**

**COOKING TIME**

## INGREDIENTS

## DIRECTIONS

## NOTES

# Recipe:

**PREP TIME**

**COOKING TIME**

## INGREDIENTS

## DIRECTIONS

## NOTES

# Recipe:

**PREP TIME**

**COOKING TIME**

## INGREDIENTS

## DIRECTIONS

## NOTES

# Recipe:

PREP TIME

COOKING TIME

## INGREDIENTS

## DIRECTIONS

## NOTES

# Recipe:

**PREP TIME**

**COOKING TIME**

## INGREDIENTS

## DIRECTIONS

## NOTES

Recipe: _____

PREP TIME ............................................ COOKING TIME ............................................

INGREDIENTS

DIRECTIONS

NOTES

# Recipe:

**PREP TIME**

**COOKING TIME**

## INGREDIENTS

## DIRECTIONS

## NOTES

# Recipe: _____

PREP TIME ............................  COOKING TIME ............................

## INGREDIENTS

## DIRECTIONS

## NOTES

# Recipe:

**PREP TIME**

**COOKING TIME**

## INGREDIENTS

## DIRECTIONS

## NOTES

# Recipe: _____

PREP TIME ......................................

COOKING TIME ......................................

## INGREDIENTS

## DIRECTIONS

## NOTES

# Recipe: _____

**PREP TIME** ....................

**COOKING TIME** ....................

## INGREDIENTS

## DIRECTIONS

## NOTES

# Recipe: _____

PREP TIME ............................. COOKING TIME .............................

## INGREDIENTS

## DIRECTIONS

## NOTES

# Recipe:

**PREP TIME** ............................................ **COOKING TIME** ............................................

## INGREDIENTS

## DIRECTIONS

## NOTES

# Recipe: _____

PREP TIME .................... COOKING TIME ....................

## INGREDIENTS

## DIRECTIONS

## NOTES

# Recipe:

**PREP TIME**

**COOKING TIME**

## INGREDIENTS

## DIRECTIONS

## NOTES

# Recipe:

**PREP TIME**

**COOKING TIME**

## INGREDIENTS

## DIRECTIONS

## NOTES

**Recipe:** _____

PREP TIME ............... COOKING TIME ...............

## INGREDIENTS

## DIRECTIONS

NOTES

# Recipe:

PREP TIME .................... COOKING TIME ....................

## INGREDIENTS

## DIRECTIONS

## NOTES

# Recipe:

PREP TIME ............................ COOKING TIME ............................

## INGREDIENTS

## DIRECTIONS

## NOTES

# Recipe: _____

**PREP TIME** ..................  **COOKING TIME** ..................

## INGREDIENTS

## DIRECTIONS

## NOTES

# Recipe:

**PREP TIME**

**COOKING TIME**

## INGREDIENTS

## DIRECTIONS

## NOTES

# Recipe:

**PREP TIME**

**COOKING TIME**

## INGREDIENTS

## DIRECTIONS

## NOTES

# Recipe:

**PREP TIME** .......... **COOKING TIME** ..........

## INGREDIENTS

## DIRECTIONS

## NOTES

# Recipe: _____

PREP TIME .................... COOKING TIME ....................

## INGREDIENTS

## DIRECTIONS

## NOTES

# Recipe:

**PREP TIME**

**COOKING TIME**

## INGREDIENTS

## DIRECTIONS

## NOTES

# Recipe:

**PREP TIME** .................... **COOKING TIME** ....................

## INGREDIENTS

## DIRECTIONS

## NOTES

# Recipe:

**PREP TIME** .................................... **COOKING TIME** ....................................

## INGREDIENTS

## DIRECTIONS

## NOTES

# Recipe:

**PREP TIME**

**COOKING TIME**

## INGREDIENTS

## DIRECTIONS

## NOTES

# Recipe: _____

PREP TIME ....................

COOKING TIME ....................

## INGREDIENTS

## DIRECTIONS

## NOTES

# Recipe:

**PREP TIME** .................... **COOKING TIME** ....................

## INGREDIENTS

## DIRECTIONS

## NOTES

# Recipe:

**PREP TIME**

**COOKING TIME**

## INGREDIENTS

## DIRECTIONS

## NOTES

# Recipe:

**PREP TIME** ............................. **COOKING TIME** .............................

## INGREDIENTS

## DIRECTIONS

## NOTES

# Recipe:

**PREP TIME** ............................

**COOKING TIME** ............................

## INGREDIENTS

## DIRECTIONS

## NOTES

Recipe: _____

........................... PREP TIME ........................... COOKING TIME

INGREDIENTS

DIRECTIONS

NOTES

Recipe: _____

PREP TIME ..........................

COOKING TIME ..........................

INGREDIENTS

DIRECTIONS

NOTES

# Recipe: _____

......................................... | .........................................
**PREP TIME** | **COOKING TIME**

## INGREDIENTS

## DIRECTIONS

## NOTES

# Recipe:

**PREP TIME** .................... **COOKING TIME** ....................

## INGREDIENTS

## DIRECTIONS

## NOTES

# Recipe: _____

PREP TIME ....................

COOKING TIME ....................

## INGREDIENTS

## DIRECTIONS

## NOTES

# Recipe:

PREP TIME

COOKING TIME

## INGREDIENTS

## DIRECTIONS

NOTES

# Recipe: _____

**PREP TIME** ..................................  **COOKING TIME** ..................................

## INGREDIENTS

## DIRECTIONS

## NOTES

# Recipe:

**PREP TIME** .................................... **COOKING TIME** ....................................

## INGREDIENTS

## DIRECTIONS

## NOTES

# Recipe: _____

PREP TIME .................... COOKING TIME ....................

## INGREDIENTS

## DIRECTIONS

## NOTES

Recipe: _____

PREP TIME .................................

COOKING TIME .................................

INGREDIENTS

DIRECTIONS

NOTES

# Recipe:

**PREP TIME**

**COOKING TIME**

## INGREDIENTS

## DIRECTIONS

## NOTES

# Recipe: _____

PREP TIME .................................... COOKING TIME ....................................

## INGREDIENTS

## DIRECTIONS

## NOTES

Recipe: _____

PREP TIME .................... COOKING TIME ....................

INGREDIENTS

DIRECTIONS

NOTES

# Recipe: _____

**PREP TIME** ....................  **COOKING TIME** ....................

## INGREDIENTS

## DIRECTIONS

## NOTES

Recipe: _____

PREP TIME .................. COOKING TIME ..................

INGREDIENTS

DIRECTIONS

NOTES

# Recipe:

**PREP TIME**

**COOKING TIME**

## INGREDIENTS

## DIRECTIONS

## NOTES

# Recipe: _____

PREP TIME ............................ COOKING TIME ............................

## INGREDIENTS

## DIRECTIONS

## NOTES

# Recipe:

**PREP TIME**

**COOKING TIME**

## INGREDIENTS

## DIRECTIONS

## NOTES

# Recipe: _____

**PREP TIME** ........................  **COOKING TIME** ........................

## INGREDIENTS

## DIRECTIONS

## NOTES

# Recipe:

**PREP TIME** .......................... **COOKING TIME** ..........................

## INGREDIENTS

## DIRECTIONS

## NOTES

# Recipe: _____

**PREP TIME** ................................ **COOKING TIME** ................................

## INGREDIENTS

## DIRECTIONS

## NOTES

Recipe: _____

PREP TIME ........................

COOKING TIME ........................

INGREDIENTS

DIRECTIONS

NOTES

Recipe: _____

PREP TIME

COOKING TIME

INGREDIENTS

DIRECTIONS

NOTES

Recipe: _____

PREP TIME ............................................

COOKING TIME ............................................

INGREDIENTS

DIRECTIONS

NOTES

# Recipe:

PREP TIME

COOKING TIME

## INGREDIENTS

## DIRECTIONS

## NOTES

# Recipe: _____

PREP TIME ......................... COOKING TIME .........................

## INGREDIENTS

## DIRECTIONS

## NOTES

# Recipe: _____

PREP TIME ..........................  COOKING TIME ..........................

## INGREDIENTS

## DIRECTIONS

## NOTES

Recipe: _____

PREP TIME ..................  COOKING TIME ..................

INGREDIENTS | DIRECTIONS

NOTES

# Recipe:

**PREP TIME**

**COOKING TIME**

## INGREDIENTS

## DIRECTIONS

## NOTES

Recipe: _____

PREP TIME .................................. COOKING TIME ..................................

## INGREDIENTS

## DIRECTIONS

## NOTES

# Recipe: _____

**PREP TIME** .................... **COOKING TIME** ....................

## INGREDIENTS

## DIRECTIONS

## NOTES

Recipe: _____

PREP TIME ............................  COOKING TIME ............................

INGREDIENTS

DIRECTIONS

NOTES

# Recipe:

**PREP TIME** .................... **COOKING TIME** ....................

## INGREDIENTS

## DIRECTIONS

## NOTES

# Recipe: _____

**PREP TIME** ..................

**COOKING TIME** ..................

## INGREDIENTS

## DIRECTIONS

## NOTES

# Recipe: _____

PREP TIME ..................................  COOKING TIME ..................................

## INGREDIENTS

## DIRECTIONS

## NOTES

# Recipe:

**PREP TIME** .................................... **COOKING TIME** ....................................

## INGREDIENTS

## DIRECTIONS

## NOTES

# Recipe:

**PREP TIME** .................... **COOKING TIME** ....................

## INGREDIENTS

## DIRECTIONS

## NOTES

**Recipe:** _____

PREP TIME

COOKING TIME

INGREDIENTS

DIRECTIONS

NOTES

# Recipe: _____

PREP TIME ........................................  COOKING TIME ........................................

## INGREDIENTS

## DIRECTIONS

## NOTES

# Recipe: _____

**PREP TIME** .................................... **COOKING TIME** ....................................

## INGREDIENTS

## DIRECTIONS

## NOTES

**Recipe:** _____

PREP TIME .................... COOKING TIME ....................

### INGREDIENTS

### DIRECTIONS

### NOTES

Made in the USA
Columbia, SC
20 January 2025